The Foundling Wheel

Also by Blas Falconer

Poetry:
A Question of Gravity and Light

As Editor:
The Other Latino: Writing Against a Singular Identity
Mentor and Muse: Essays from Poets to Poets

The Foundling Wheel

Blas Falconer

Four Way Books

Tribeca

Please direct all inquiries to:
Editorial Office
Four Way Books
POB 535, Village Station
New York, NY 10014
www.fourwaybooks.com

Library of Congress Cataloging-in-Publication Data

Falconer, Blas.
  [Poems. Selections]
  The foundling wheel / Blas Falconer.
      pages cm
  ISBN 978-1-884800-98-6 (pbk.)
  I. Title.
  PS3606.A425F68 2012
  811'.6--dc23

                            2012002005

This book is manufactured in the United States of America
and printed on acid-free paper.

Four Way Books is a not-for-profit literary press. We are grateful for the assistance
we receive from individual donors, public arts agencies, and private foundations.

This publication is made possible with public funds
from the National Endowment for the Arts

and from the New York State Council on the Arts, a state agency.

We are a proud member
of the Council of Literary Magazines and Presses.

Distributed by University Press of New England
One Court Street, Lebanon, NH 03766

Contents

For Joseph and for Rane
For my father

To press the air, to bless the silhouette,

the owl and the field mice—that argument—
and spare no speck of dust or fleck of light,

all fair and foul, lush and bare: the vine
that takes the barn, the nest inside the brush

(the dog's muzzle soaked in blood);
to resist caving in, taking comfort

in routine, facts sorted, shrinking from
disorder; to cut the fruit and not think

of the heart, to think of it and not flinch,
or flinch and cut through its core all the same,

you wake up, walk out late at night still dazed,
and stand in the yard, which, at day, lolls

under heat, the red trumpet blossoms bob,
where, at dusk, strays rise from the tall grass

to wander streets, a fearless pack
in search of food among the trash you've left

exposed. Below, the city rests. You'll test
yourself the way you always have, a boy

stepping into the dark and the story
it held—whatever it was.

The Annunciation

Whether she lifts a hand to her breast in protest or
surprise, I can't say, though we know how it ends.

He reaches out as if to keep her there, her fingers on
the open book of prayer or song, the cloth draped

across her waist. *Faith*, he might have said
as the cells of disbelief began to multiply: a son

who'd face great pain? Certain death? In one account,
she fled. He chased her back into the house,

not Gabriel, a pull inside the ribs until
she acquiesced, exchanging one loss for another.

X-rays expose a sign of someone else's brush.
Experts doubt the dress or wings are his

but claim the sleeve, the buttoned cuff, a triumph,
young as the artist was, not having found

perspective: the vanishing point too high, one hand
too large, the flaw in her face: a lack of fear or awe.

On the Bluffs of Pico Duarte

I climb the cliff despite its slope,
    my wet feet, your voice

calling me back (*Because I want*
    you to live forever, you say,

later) and leap into the river,
    braiding down the mountainside.

I fall—a blur of rock and branch,
    the boat of faces—pierce

the water, sink deep, so my legs
    wander the bottom, so

the halo of light begins to close.
    I like the cold and muted dark,

the stillness there, but the lungs
    want, too, and I think of you

above, leaning over the edge,
    holding your breath, and kick

at the emptiness below. That night
    you take a bath and crawl in bed.

Why? You ask, and close your eyes,
　　even this small lamp too bright.

Saved

We knelt around her chair, letters hung

    in pairs about the room, and two men

climbed a cliff in the book she read. One

    wouldn't *make it*, she said, but meant

the man who didn't die, and God became

    a place you went if the body became

too much to bear—irony the lesson

    humming at night. We marched to the door,

but I'd come back, reaching down to save

    my father from a deadly fall. *Catch me*,

I call to the bedside clock, a bare wall.

Still Life with Orange

The fruit on the plate is split in two.

An open hand holds the air
or the shadow of the head that hangs above.

The window gives a square of light.

Someone may be crying there:
a white blossom. This end looks

like the human navel
because a second fruit fails

to grow within the first.
The seedless fruit cannot bear fruit.

It sings in the mouth of one.

In Medias Res

At six months, the embryo
        can hear, its eyes close
and open on the crease—
        fingernails and hair.

We tape green swatches to the wall
        and settle on a name
(though that, too, will change).

Dogs whine and claw the door.
        Each day calls for rain.
We wonder: the face, the weight,
        the size of his swaddled frame.

~

Standing on the curb at dusk,
        I sweep my hand
through the mailbox built
        in the shape of a birdhouse.

Among clover and chickweed,
        it lies, slumped over,
a mound of feather breaking down

to jointed bone. Fireflies
        hover through the empty field
in the absence of light and hunger—
        without news or song.

Another Point of View

Think of her trip outside the city,
months of hiding—a room so small
she crammed the mattress in
and left the box spring on the street.

She lay there while the world
pulsed against her window: a stoplight
on its timer, cars braking, a song
she'd like to sing, fading out.

At night she dreamt a bubble born
from her open mouth: *No*, she said
to the dark, and the word floated up,
so even the air belonged to her.

The Foundling Wheel

i.

They swept the river, caught the dead
      in nets. Then a wheel with a box
let someone leave a child. As boats sway
      beneath the wall, their loose cords

swing and clank the hollow masts,
      so the masts call out like dulled bells.
At low tide, their hulls lie in mud.
      A mother rolls her stroller back and forth,

looking at—the rain? My mind drifts at night,
      the current rising on the bank,
the sound of water splashing from the roof.

      The blue curtain glows at dawn.
I hear the gulls and don't sleep well.

ii.

The one who set her son adrift
        must have stood among the reeds
as long as she could. The hand that throws
        the stone recalls its weight.

A father's body changes, too,
        on a molecular level:
a small disturbance among fallen leaves,
        a soft thud. A stream of light

at dawn, the bells ring and ring,
        the world's wheel turning toward
this, the 6th day of October:

        the child sleeps beside our bed
and you make toast with red plum jam.

Homecoming

Rain against the roof sounds like a slow tire
over gravel, as if a friend has come.
The train rumbles through the dark, and my body, tuned
to hear you cry before you cry, stirs.

The lamp floats in the window, the only window lit
at this late hour on the empty street.
Your hands unfurl as you fall asleep.

Small Clock of Needs, Law that I Abide,
the leaves gloss and shine. Like this we rock
and sink into the long night of our rocking.

A Warm Day in Winter

The leash looped around my wrist, we stop
to let the dog piss across a trunk—
the branches stark this late in winter,
though everyone is out, spreading blankets
on the grass, eating with plastic forks.
We amble across the park without purpose
or direction, our wheels pausing
at stick and stone before we jostle on,
your eyes attuned to every first, fixed
upon the few leaves above, withered
but holding. You flail your fists
at the small sky, the brief light it carries.
Tomorrow, the cold will rush back
into the city, and neither you nor the dog
will understand or remember, though
you might respond cheerfully, not knowing why,
when we return one day in spring. I try
to see as you, without likeness or memory,
as I did the night that you were born.
Before, I couldn't guess your complexion,
the color of your eyes, the mark that spread
across your back like a map of the world.
I told myself it was because you didn't come
from me, but Mother says it was the same
for her. At once, the thought became the form
as in the myth, the woman springs
from her father's head, your face determined
in its particulars, the forehead's frown
beneath lamps that kept you warm, the hoarse cry

as you expelled the first breaths of air,
so in my arms, at last, I didn't know you
but looked in wonder all the same,
noting how little you weighed. You will not
recall any of this, of course, which seems
a shame, when you are older, how
I fed you through the late hours in a room,
sterile and cold, but for paintings of landscapes
much like this one or how we walked
along the row of trees avoiding roots
that surfaced, and stopped awhile
beneath an elm on a warm December day.

Vertigo

When I spin, our son laughs louder, his weight
growing in my arms, and the window streaks
across my field of view, so it becomes indistinct
from the vase on the table, also full of light.

The lilies' stems vanish, so the blossoms seem
to float in air. As we slow, the room finds itself
once more, and you, against the door, laughing, too.

The night your father died, you told me how
he saved your life, twice dunking your fevered body
in a tub of ice, and we lay still in the quiet dark.

When I stop, our son's voice, the spirit, the impulse
toward joy, fills the room, but you are far away again.
Dizzy, breathless, we walk to you as if to cross
the great deck of a ship at sea—stumble, sway, tip.

Field Marks for Western Birds

Joseph blows, so the film expands,
and you wait for it to part
from the serrated ring.

It may perch on the tip of a reed,
light as it is—delicate
as the mobile above your crib.

You pull the string to make
it fly. He sings, surprised how long
it rains and also when it stops.

Wrists small, fingers pale
and fine—*Bird, bird*, you say,
the bubble breaking in your hands.

~

You hear an engine in the sky
and point to the belly of the plane,
throw stones in a plastic pool,
cup water in your hands.

Joseph's gone, but he'll be back.
Last night, you kissed his face
and flipped the frame to find
it blank. You see a car that looks

like his and make the sign:
Father. Waves splash the rim,
I pass the towel. You seem
surprised—how wet you've gotten.

~

As I laid you down, it began to rain
and because he left the window open,
I turned from you, who slept, and went to pull

it shut, but the cover gave a bit,
so it seemed all right, after all—one shaft
of light, the floor dry thanks to eaves above.

Drops fell across the glass tabletop outside,
and in the grass, a black bird preened
itself, shaking water from its wings, so when

it flew, I thought, *Now, you'll never know,*
but caught a glimpse of the iridescent head,
fantail spread, and knew what kind it was.

Still Life with Three Zinnia Elegans

If each bloom is a step in the story, the photograph a point of view, then this flower in the forefront is my fevered son in lamplight, his face lit brightest, whom I lay in bed, clearing away the sheets, standing over him.

The stem must have stirred to make the digital glitch, the blossom's blur.

Too much light, perhaps, too much time exposed to light, so where the petals pull across the frame, there is color, there in the error—blue and yellow.

First, he stiffened. Then shook, eyelids aflutter, and a groan that could have meant my name.

A girl bit the tip of her mother's finger off, the doctor once warned.

It seemed to go on forever, this argument.

When it ended, it ended at once, his whole self, I thought, leaving his body or sinking deeper into it.

I placed a hand on his chest—his face calm unlike before when all I could do was watch.

You Try and Hope You're Wrong

As I drowned, Mother stepped into the sea
        somewhere else. Boats split against the surf,
the helicopter crisscrossed the Mona Pass
        till nightfall. I shine a beam into the brush.

The first frost, and the cat's been gone for days.
        When the neighbor's dog gave birth, the last
of three lay still on the blood-smeared floor.
        She licked until the membrane tore. I thought,

It never works this way. I pulled myself
        onto the dock. By morning, shoes washed ashore.
A girl who went to sleep hungry woke up
        in bed with half a sandwich in her hand—

on her cheek, a sticky film that tasted like
        strawberries. I wonder where she is. I can
almost hear her, but branches rock, dropping
        all their leaves at once, and the wind won't help.

Attic

The dimmest light is the only light
    that works—the brass bed frame
against the wall, the dresser drawer
    full of knobs. The sound of fan blades

in the vent wheel is the sound
    of a nest above the still air.
You hesitate over the heap
    of your inheritance. The way

you close your eyes to feel
    your way around a room at night
is how you might miss

    someone, forget what you are
looking for: the lamp's beaded pull
    is the sound of the dark in your hand.

Look at You

The photo disappoints because you didn't know

   what you wanted—not

the image of the horse's head bending down,

   but the tenderness when his mouth

took the apple from your hand—

     that it wouldn't end so soon.

Not the fallen branch after the storm.

      Not hair caught on barbs,

or woven in the nest above the door.

The wren sank into that pocket of twigs and moss.

Only yesterday, you stood in beds of purple flowers,

    thinking: *This, too, is the world,*

   the mint leaf, absurdly sweet.

As if to touch, now, the shards of small eggs,

scattered like petals, at first, like confetti,

the yolks still wet,

        you bend to the ground.

     You will not find it there

either, tenderness, but someone might

     in a face transformed beyond recognition

though you have known it all your life.

Maybe I'm Not Here at All

Two cars crash, the drivers thrown to either side
of the road. They lie in the dark for hours

before anyone finds them. Until then,
all one has is the other and the occasion:

a cough of blood, a kind of drowning.
They will each other to live without a word.

When I was young, a bus ran into a tree,
and children flew for the first time,

their hands open and stretched in front of them.
Even the long seats, bolted down, tipped,

pinning one boy. One bled from his head, one
from her thigh. They pulled us out and set

us down in the field, the grass, cold and wet
on my back. My brother bent over me

to say, *If the engine blows* . . . , and rushed
into the woods. The maple's orange fringe,

its red heart. The shallow sky. Could this
be true? They sawed the driver's head free

from the wheel. I remember her brown curls.
I loved her. When I closed my eyes, I heard

a valve hiss, a whimper. You fall asleep, first.
You turn and stir. You breathe the heavy air.

After You've Been Gone a Long Time

There are no rubies here, but saying so brings one to mind. And they aren't petals as much as one furled bud with a very long stem.

Ants take everything away, little by little, before you know.

You came home briefly, for instance, and I was asleep, so it was as though you hadn't come at all, but something was missing.

More time, I thought, might be like more water and make it taste less bitter, but only made it more to drink.

Sometimes, I can't bear waiting. If you were here, you'd see what I mean, someone staring off all the time.

Once, when I fell, my mother gasped, which only made me cry louder, and people gathered to see fear that looked like pain. That's what I'm trying to say.

The neighbors mow the yard, and it sounds like a plane overhead where everything is clear.

Palimpsest

A near square corded off with twine,
the stalks staked and circled by wire,
my father sprayed a mist at dawn.
With time, the air sprang solid,
a tangle of sweet, spiders webbing wheels
from leaf to leaf, fattened bulbs,
green and red, twisted from the stem.
Summer of hands, fork and shovel,
summer of coiled hose, spigot's crank,
the house's shadow crossed the yard.
We stacked them in bowls, filled
paper bags, spread seeds over the plot,
so grass wove one bed, edge to edge,
even in color, as if, the fruit long gone,
nothing else had ever grown there.

Passing

Little labels at the market, peppers strung
above the door, a pinch of paprika
on every table, the year I lived alone.
The ducks long gone, snowdrifts blocked

the road. When tiles fell from shower stalls,
I thought, *Dinner plates*—the way they sounded,
crashing to the floor. One night, girls stood
below the balcony, singing up, faces like

saucers, round and white. A webbed foot
in a bowl of soup was a sign of good luck.
What could I say while others sighed with envy,
the small bones breaking in my mouth.

Another Kind of Music

1.

I climbed the hill where a man lived with a man who mowed the lawn
on Sundays. Even from across the street, you could see his jockstrap
when he bent to pull the cord or empty grass from the carriage. I doubt
he saw me chasing birds in his yard with a handful of salt. Scott's dad
wanted to live with a man, but didn't tell anyone for years, and I didn't
tell anyone though my father often asked me what was wrong. More
bird talk, more twitter. Didn't we all want one? You had to catch it
first. You had to make it understand.

2.

When my sister played piano, I lay on the floor with a book, looking up through the glass tabletop.

The figurine swung a basket of flowers and shook out her hair.

I never would have guessed, all the little hammers.

Outside, vines wrapped around the trellis that my father built and painted the same shade of red as the house and mailbox. Grapes grew small and taut, too sour to eat, though we tried each year.

A car drove by, which sounded like another kind of music.

My mother sat still for as long as she could.

I read, *The history of the Earth cannot be explained.*

It rained for millions and millions and millions of years.

3.

Others gathered around and led my father from the edge of the lake.

I couldn't explain why—how I wanted to see the look of wonder on his face as grains floated down, dimpling the surface—much as they asked.

He bent over and held his hands to his eyes.

It made little sense after the fact.

They held a cup over his tipped head, and a small stream ran down as he blinked, letting light and water in.

Someone pointed to a square of grass, where I sat and brushed the sand still stuck to my fingers.

The boat bumped the pier and pulled against the rope. I didn't consider the wind.

Ice bobbed in the chest, banging against the Styrofoam walls, as he carried it back to the picnic table.

We started over. I opened all the gifts. We ate cake and sipped bright orange soda from paper cups.

He crumpled wrapping and ribbons and shoved them into garbage bags. He stacked boxes in order of their size.

4.

May, June, July: it sloshed in waves at low tide, weeds climbed the
fence but didn't bloom. As girls spun in chairs with rollers in their hair,
Pilar sewed another dress, and the pinball shot from a spring—flash,
ping—fell down a chute. The tortoise rose for air, and the neighbor's
boy took off his clothes. *Tortuga*, someone yelled, pointing from the
boat. The word sang like water from a hose.

5.

It was your job to stand behind me, hands on my waist, ready to lift me up, count *1, 2*—.

First, I had to see myself, you said, grip change and release, start to end, the way a stranger might, but I couldn't get it right: the hollow chest or arched back, the toe point, always forgetting something, something else wanting in.

You remained calm, looking up.

You lifted the warehouse doors to let air in, and letting go, I rose high into it, above blue mats, not knowing where my body was, my hands slipping or the bar out of reach.

The difference between what happened and what I thought would happen, I could never account for.

It takes time to learn how the body turns, spotting the floor in a blur of lights.

I gave up in mid flight.

I fell short or long.

There was little you could do.

6.

I loved how everything seemed to hold the light, and noted how later
tired from holding the light—the trees, for example, bending a little.

Leaning my head against the glass, dreaming, I thought, *It's just a kiss,
a little kiss in the dark.*

I recalled her leotard with the ruffle skirt that she washed by hand in
the sink.

Above the door, it said, EXIT, in red letters.

Also, white skates with pink laces. You had to move the tongue around
and around with your eyes closed.

One year led to the next, kiss after kiss.

I was always not there, much as I tried, so you had to look for me in the
other place.

You had to wave your arms or rest a hand on my shoulder.

Stray

I grabbed his scruff and led him to the car,
lifted him with both arms—the way
I carry wood for the fire. He didn't fight

as if he understood. I wondered what—
a bat or pipe?—could make a break so clean.

And who? And why? He slumps to the floor,
I tug the leash, a diamond of light falls
from the window. Everything here is hard:

a plastic chair with metal legs. *I'll pay*,
I say, *no matter what*, and wonder how.

Song

They set the bone
     and pin the plate,

sew the skin
     and tell me how

your leg will heal:
     Awkward at best.

Even the acrobat
     who gains a pound

or grows an inch
     throws the physics off.

You must walk with care,
     less jumping down,

less dreaming. But
     speckled birds

sail across the lawn,
     and the steady growl

that never seems
     to start or end

grows loud enough
     to hear. The birds

rise and fall
        again. You shake

and pull the leash.
        Your body sings

this song and breaks
        when I let you go.

Infidelity

In the flashing light of an otherwise dark club,
in the charged air (so the tiny hairs tremble),
someone kissed a man. That wasn't the point.

In our own stone house, the dog caught the cat
in his mouth. For days you wouldn't look
but thought, *He swung him side to side, the floor
covered with fur.* You wipe the counters clean,

dry your hands on the back of your jeans.
Swimming laps, I think of him and go under,
of before, small joys accumulating each day,
adding to what was there. *So much fur,*

I didn't think there could be so much fur.
I ran my hand the length of him,
noting no hum of life, the tip of his pale tongue,
and where the bite broke the skin—the lungs

filled up with blood. I slip the box on the shelf,
hear ashes shift and know how fine they are.
He licks salt from my palm. He rolls
onto his back, and I stroke his tender belly.

We lie side by side. We wait and wonder.
While he sleeps, we hear the body rise and fall.

If

Years later, you still wonder. Had only you kissed
that morning, everything would

be different now: train routes,
the way rain falls into the field for months,

your calloused heels. When did you grow
so tall? Maybe the walk would have been

shorter/longer, the letters home
less/more frequent—hours in the phone booth

calling out as others paced the dark,
pulling their coats closed, bowing their heads

to the wind. Where is he now, the other young man
written in no book? Where you left him,

asleep, half dressed. Smokestacks stretch
into the sky of every city.

This is the cause of all your pain
and joy, neither of which lasts long.

The Lotus Eaters

In November I think of the long drive home.
If I spoke, she rolled her eyes and stared out the window.

I ran my fingertips along her forearm,
and the hem of her plaid skirt swayed above her knees

as she walked from the car. In her house, with its flat roof
and glass doors, its green shag and the rotting deck

that looked onto the woods, she cut my hair,
and we turned cartwheels on the strip of tape

that stretched across the floor. We dipped our feet
in the plastic pool and wondered where

our friends had gone. Her mother cooked
pumpkin soup, and we built a fire.

She threw blankets down, and we leaned in,
blowing on the flames. Outside, the sky filled with smoke

and the smell of burning wood. The trees stood
silent and dark, the birds of winter

settled on the grass. Inside, we dimmed the lights
and gathered around with cake in our hands, singing.

When she turned the knob of that heavy door,

the seal broke—the sound of a kiss—
to the dark outside, a small lamp
lighting the steps, the smell of grapes
nearly ripe and sandstones spread below.

The neighbor's voice filled the house,
a voice I knew but couldn't name,
didn't know possible, this *wailing*,
the best word, I thought later, *without*

reservation, so she seemed completely
herself, my friend, and greater than that,
utterly human, and therefore could be
anyone or everyone—her father dead.

Another Round

When Joseph sings, you sing
in perfect pitch—the note
he makes, you make without
much thought—rising

from your chest, rising
from your open throat.
When Joseph sings, you sing
in perfect pitch—his note

grows in dimension
and design, paired with yours.
I wish that I were more
prepared for this:
when Joseph sings, you sing.

A Letter Home

I got the box of books and found the pics
between the pages. Thanks. I see how hard
it must have been for you to be so far
from home. The view can take my mind off it—
the buds about to leaf, Big Horns capped
in ice. With bills to pay, we had no choice,
but it was tough waking up alone,
the boy asking where you'd gone. At least
I got to be with him. It rains a lot.
The creek will rise above the bank,
where grackles live in brush and bramble.
When I was young, I'd venture in the woods
behind my father's house, where cattails grew
in muck, and pines along the hill—for hours
walking there, oblivious to time. A path
leads from the drive across the un-mowed grass.
I like to hike along the edge. I found
a nest, and then a meadowlark (I saw
its yellow breast) cried out. When he got sick,
I let him sleep with me and bathed him in
the kitchen sink, where sunlight from
the window kept him warm. You know all this,
I know you know all this. Kiss his face
for me and pet the dog a bit each day.
When I get back, we'll take them both
to Percy Warner Park. We'll eat and swim.
At night, the wind could be the sea outside.
I come around and wonder where I am.

A Common Ground

To find the fixed point
from which everything is

perceived—the stitch
that holds a hem or joins

two ends to keep. The geese
can fly, but let the spot

from which you hear the geese
remain, the mountain range

take half the sky
inside the window frame.

Eclogue: An Argument

Say, *brush*, and I see nothing but brush, and if you say, *river*, then let the river divide the brush in two. How deep must a river be to not be a creek, and can a creek be a river part of the year after snow melts on the mountain or heavy rain? Perhaps, a river is defined—not by depth, but the distance between two banks or the volume of water that enters another body of water. Who decides? A green hill rises on the other side, much like the hill on this side. Behind the hills are more hills, I imagine, and beyond that, I really can't say.

It begins with

a silver faucet, a salt shaker
on the window sill. I must go
if I want to take you with me.
You've lived here
longer than I've lived
anywhere. Think warm bread,
think fire. Then something more stable,
more lasting, a table or chair.
From there, it builds itself:
the walls, a roof, the world outside,
four dogs, and ten
acres of trees. It's cold.
Today, let's call it a farmhouse.
You say, *Maybe a barn painted red.*
We build it together, which
is what I meant by *Better.*

Deus Ex Machina

Think of exits, stage lefts, of a small key hidden under the tongue, the frayed knot or the pocket of air, room for one more. The man who fell overboard—carried on the back of a turtle, how unbelievable, yet one can't help think of the figure floating in the ocean, waving as the ship comes for him days later. A man said of friends who'd died: *Stupid*, pointing to each framed face, as if life were merely a matter of wit and will. Didn't a prophet rise into heaven whole because God loved him so? A mural of clouds parted—and what did his companion think, standing among stones where only the night before, they had slept together? Tell another story. Hang pillowed stars, suspended by string, above the crib.

the way the boys danced,
stomping the ground, and clapped

the fluorescent air. Wasps nested
in the overgrowth—the hum

rising over the house. Your parents sat
on the balcony, drinking wine,

and their laughter fell.
It would be this forever: all their hands

glittering in the dark. You had
no words, sobbing for every one.

~

You don't know how
you got here, to this kindness. You know

the rabbits tremble in their wire cages,
fine bones beneath the prairie fur,

long, soft ears. Jam cools in jars
on the shelf. You speak the few words you know

and shake your head,
pointing to maps on the wall.

Every face becomes strange, less human,
more beautiful. You set

the water glass down
and head back to the brush, rested,

reaching out to the dark, testing each step,
giving in to the ground.

Lighter,

the word that comes to mind after many nights.
As when a plane descends over a city
you call home, the body's rise against the belt
strung across your lap. Darkness and lampposts,
like gold and silver beads below, falling
into them. Or better yet, wading in
the bioluminescent bay and each kick
creates a soft glow, each stroke makes you think
light could come from the body, and not
a world disturbed into brilliance. Because
it captures what I mean—both the weight
and how you see what you could not. As when
I heard him cry and lumbered down the hall
to find you there, first, pacing the room, singing
softly in his ear. Through the window,
the city sparkled and seemed to have grown
though, by day, I never see more than two
or three men working at once, lifting
together, say, a plank of wood. Years ago,
my mother sat beside my bed, eager to bear
the fever with me. We pass him back
and forth between us till it breaks,
and I no longer want what I wanted
before. As when one day you look upon
the house you've built and can't recall the field.

How to Tell a Story

We stood on either side and took turns crossing—first, slowly, in a
dead hang.

Her father, who taught me how to ride a bike, holding the back of my
seat, running beside me—if she said, *He can't come out,* or nothing at
all, you understood as much.

We learned to swing from one rung to the next, stretching out in
anticipation.

The dog paced the fence. He lay in sunlight or circled the yard.

Before long, we could skip a bar and reach each other faster, which is
how you might tell a story.

She kept the *Speak Chinese* tapes and practiced all spring.

The grass grew longer.

Hello, Goodbye, and *Thank you very much.*

Kneeling down, we hugged his neck, held his paw to our faces.

You could smell the whole afternoon there.

You Will Like It Here

Let it be too-early light, your first
memory, the dog lapping from
the water bowl. I eat and make my way

across the gravel path, a handful of stones.
Let it be among these birds
and other birds. She said, *The hardest thing*

I have done, and changed her mind
more than once. There is no word
for the way your mother touched you,

you must know—and four
brothers somewhere. *The hardest thing*,
and left. You must know that there

were tears, nothing we won't do—
of that you can be sure. The window looks
upon a field, three horses grazing in the rain.

A Proof

This yard is sacred. Our son
reaches into the sky and cups the moon to his mouth.
When I close my eyes, the color makes
me think of his blanket, the great cosmos,

the Big Bang, how before, the void ate light,
matter, time—there was no limit to that hunger.
Turned under the streetlamp, the rock's bright specks
look infinite. In a multiverse, he is here,
holding his small hand to his face, and he

is not here. Beyond one edge, a new world
imagines itself expanding in air.
We lean back in the grass. The leap
is cold and dark. The lungs open and open again.

On Joy

The horse bends to what's fallen, the branch
lifting, as fowl fly overhead
to the thing they've waited for
among reeds, all winter, and dragonflies.

The horse fattens on what it's been
denied these months, watching buds
flower and wilt, the apple swell
beyond its capacity for fullness, the stem's

small knot. Why long for what will soon
be gone if there is no happiness
like the one passing now?

Moths flutter near the mare's mouth,
so the air about her face blooms
briefly with small, white blossoms.

Adaptation

The air grows warmer, the tidal pool
more shallow over time.

On the sand, each shell cups an ocean
long after it dies (the birds above)

and jellies shine like bubbles among the stones.
The challenge rises,

stubborn and wordless—the instinct to do
what can't be done:

to carry themselves
a few feet. Last night they rocked

through the dark sea
which brought them here.

~

It's not a story you can tell.
Fireflies pulsed in the night sky.

Someone kicked a bucket of tadpoles
in the grass, and a small lamp

lit the tent you pitched in the backyard.
You weren't prepared—

Notes

"*The Annunciation*" is in response to Leonardo da Vinci's painting with the same title.

"The Foundling Wheel": "The first foundling wheel, a rotating platform, dates from 1198. It was installed in the wall of the Santo Spirito Hospital near the Vatican on orders from Pope Innocent III. He'd been dismayed by the number of newborns found caught in the nets of fishermen on the Tiber River." Sylvia Poggioli's NPR article, "Italy Takes High-Tech Tactics for Abandoned Babies," published March 7, 2007.

"Still Life with Three Zinnia Elegans" is in response to a photograph by Bruce Checefsky.

"Look at You" is in response to a photograph by Tulu Bayar.

Acknowledgments

Some of these poems (or versions of them) appeared in the
following journals:
Adirondack Review, *Ariel*, *Blue Mesa Review*, *Connotation*,
Country Dog Review, *Crab Orchard Review*, *Descant*,
The Hampden-Sydney Poetry Review, *Iron Horse Literary Review*,
Knockout, *Luna*, *Matter*, *Nashville Review*, *Ocho*, *Palabra*,
Puerto Del Sol, *Whiskey Island Magazine*, and *Yalobusha Review*.

"Still Life with Three Zinnias Elegans" first appeared in the literature/
art collaborative project: *Show and Tell*: http://031454a.netsolhost.com/
inquire/category/artistsandwriters/

This book could not have been written without the generous support
of the National Endowment for the Arts, the Center of Excellence for
the Creative Arts, Austin Peay State University, Virginia Center for
the Creative Arts, Poets and Writers and the Maureen Egen Writers
Exchange, The Jentel Foundation, and The Tennessee Arts Commission.
I would also like to thank Martha Rhodes and the other editors at
Four Way Books for their guidance and commitment to this project.
Finally, for their encouragment and support, I offer my deepest
gratitude to family, friends, and colleagues, including Daniel Blasi,
Lisa D. Chávez, Stephanie Dugger, Paul Guest, David Keplinger,
Lorraine López, Beth Martinelli, Helena Mesa, Sharon Muñiz,
June Yang, and, of course, Joseph Cassell.

Blas Falconer is the author of *A Question of Gravity and Light* and a coeditor of two essay collections, *The Other Latino: Writing Against a Singular Identity* and *Mentor and Muse: Essays from Poets to Poets*. The recipient of an NEA Fellowship, the Maureen Egen Writers Exchange, and a Tennessee Individual Artist Grant, his poems have appeared in various literary journals, including *Crab Orchard Review*, *Hampden-Sydney Poetry Review*, and *Puerto del Sol*. He is the Coordinator for the Creative Writing Program at Austin Peay State University and the poetry editor at *Zone 3 Journal* / Zone 3 Press.